CONTENTS

Welcome to Fort Nelson, the Royal Armouries museum of artillery – one of the last great fortresses ever built in Britain.

Fort Nelson was constructed in the 1860s to protect Britain from an invasion that many feared would be mounted by a resurgent French Empire. Its design was intended to give it the firepower to stop the enemy capturing the vital naval stronghold of Portsmouth.

That war never came, but Fort Nelson would go on to play its part in the First World War and, most notably, in the Second World War when it helped to see off another possible invasion – this time by the Germans.

Over 70 years later Fort Nelson remains the best preserved Victorian fort of its type, giving you the chance to explore its barracks, guardroom, tunnels and ramparts, discover the story of the fort in its fascinating galleries, and get close to the big guns that could have subjected the enemy to such devastating fire.

Home of the Big Guns

Today Fort Nelson also houses the artillery collection of the Royal Armouries – the national museum of arms and armour, which also has two other sites, one in Leeds and the other at the Tower of London. In fact, you can see a piece of stone from the Tower of London built into the entrance of Fort Nelson's visitor centre.

The extraordinary riches of the Royal Armouries collection makes Fort Nelson one of the finest showcases for artillery anywhere in the world. Only here can you see so many big guns spanning so many centuries of conflict, conquest and technological prowess. And only here can you combine that experience with the visceral thrill of seeing, hearing and feeling some of these tremendous guns in action.

We hope you enjoy your visit to the Royal Armouries at Fort Nelson, and we look forward to welcoming you back.

Fort Nelson is complex by design, with an asymmetrical shape that almost defies description. As you begin your visit, it helps to understand the reasons behind this complexity, which reveal much about the role that the fort was built to perform.

Fort Nelson was designed to mount the most effective defence possible of Portsmouth, taking into account the local topography and its place in the chain of new forts planned to stand alongside it on the ridge. According to the military thinking in vogue at the time, this meant a fortification that ran over several interlocking levels bordered by outer walls of irregular lengths, heights and angles. This was so that guns of different types and sizes could be employed to provide long, medium and short-range fire with as wide or as narrow a focus as required. This capability, combined with the fields of fire of the other forts, meant that there would be no pockets of 'dead ground' in the surrounding countryside in which the enemy could escape attack from either the front or the flank. As a further defensive measure, the fort had a deliberately low profile, so that its ramparts were not much higher than the contours of the hillside, making it difficult for the enemy to see and even more difficult to hit.

Little of this complexity can be guessed at as you approach the fort from the road, nor even as you cross the drawbridge to enter within its walls. In fact, even if you climb up to the highest level of the ramparts, it is difficult to get an accurate sense of how the whole structure fits together.

▲ The east upper entrance to Fort Nelson.

◀ *Opposite:* Mallet's Mortar. xix.286

Get your bearings

Many visitors find it helpful to discover that Fort Nelson was designed to prevent an attack on Portsmouth from inland – from the north, east or west – by an invading force that had landed elsewhere along the coast. It is useful to bear in mind then that the imposing walls you can see as you approach from the road make up the south face of the fort – the coastal side that would have been furthest away from any attack. As you head from the visitor centre and cross the drawbridge, you are therefore entering the rear of the fort – at the base of what can loosely be described as a blunted arrowhead.

Follow your interests

People choose to come to the Royal Armouries at Fort Nelson for a wide variety of reasons, some drawn by the chance to find out more about the fort's history, some wanting to explore its ramparts, defences and tunnels, some wanting to see the nation's greatest artillery treasures up close, and others wanting to do all this and more.

Whatever you want to see and explore, your starting point will be the Voice of the Guns gallery – the display space you enter when you first cross the drawbridge. Laid out over two floors, it houses some of the finest and most interesting pieces in the Royal Armouries collection.

From here, there are three main aspects of the fort that visitors tend to concentrate on, all of which are given their own section in this guidebook.

▲ The entrance level of the Voice of the Guns gallery.

The Story of Fort Nelson (see page 12)

From the lower floor of the Voice of the Guns gallery, you can explore what used to be the barracks building, which runs along the rear wall of the fort. This now houses galleries telling the Story of Fort Nelson, reconstructions of some of the original Victorian rooms, and exhibitions exploring what it was like to be garrisoned here. It is a story of military service that stretches from the 1860s through to the end of the Second World War – with evidence of the latter especially visible on the graffiti-covered walls of the guardroom and cells in the south-west corner of the fort.

▲ The east upper entrance.

How Fort Nelson worked (see page 34)

Running along the outside of the barracks building is the street, which is a great place to begin exploring how Fort Nelson worked as a defensive structure, taking in the tunnels, the underground magazine, the North Mortar Battery, the light guns mounted in the North Caponier, the Parade, and the big guns emplaced on the ramparts.
You can reach the street either by making your way through the galleries in the barracks building, or by walking directly through the Voice of the Guns gallery and heading outside to where steps to the left can take you down to street level.

▲ The North Caponier flanking gallery.

The Royal Armouries Collection (see page 48)

Explore almost any section of Fort Nelson and you will come across a range of outstanding exhibits from the Royal Armouries' collection of artillery. The Voice of the Guns gallery is a great starting point if you want to make this the focus of your visit. From there, you can then head directly outside and make your way forward to the massive Artillery Hall, where guns from across the ages and continents stand side by side. More guns are exhibited on the open ground of the Parade, and you can go on to explore galleries in the barracks building, which present the chronological Story of Artillery.

▲ The German '88' and British 3.7 inch anti-aircraft guns. XIX.331 and XIX.840

See the highlights

If time is short, or you want to get a taste of all three aspects of what Fort Nelson has to offer, there are a variety of exhibits and experiences that you simply should not miss.

If guns are your primary interest, do not miss those shown opposite.

7 *Site map.* Examine the graffiti in the guardroom left behind by soldiers stationed here during the Second World War.

Outside Fort Nelson

23 *Site map.* The towering monument to Admiral Horatio Nelson, which predates the fort and inspired its name.

3 *Site map.* Enjoy the many wonders of the Voice of the Guns gallery.

9 *Site map.* Experience the daily gun firing at 1pm.

24 *Site map.* The squat profile of Mallet's Mortar, the largest bore mortar ever built, capable of hurling a 1-ton bomb high into the air over enemy lines.

6 *Site map.* Explore the eerie depths of the main tunnel and underground magazines.

13 *Site map.* Take in the views and heavy artillery mounted on the ramparts.

25 *Site map.* The enormous 14-inch battleship gun, capable of hitting a target 22 miles away.

The Voice of the Guns

Great Turkish Bombard
See page 55

German '88'
See page 65

Iraqi 'Supergun'
See page 68

The Story of Artillery

Boxted Bombard
See page 54

Henrician saker
See page 57

Art of Artillery

Furies gun
See page 46

Ramparts

64-pounder gun
See page 44

Parade

'Cherbourg' bronze gun
See page 50

Artillery Hall

British 18-pounder field gun
See page 63

THE STORY OF FORT NELSON

In the galleries housed in the barrack buildings of Fort Nelson, you can find exhibitions and reconstructions that bring the history of the fortification to life. They start by addressing the question of why Fort Nelson was built.

The Story of Fort Nelson

When the first troops marched into Fort Nelson in 1871, they were entering one of the most remarkable forts ever built in Britain – part of a massive ring of new brick, masonry and earth fortifications designed to protect Britain from the threat of invasion.

To understand this threat, you need only consider the Nelson Monument which had stood sentinel on this part of Portsdown Hill for sixty-three years – and which still stands outside the fort today. It was erected during the Napoleonic Wars to commemorate Admiral Horatio Nelson, killed while defeating the combined French and Spanish naval forces at the Battle of Trafalgar in 1805. Nelson secured a vital victory in the war against Emperor Napoleon I of France, whose threat to Britain was finally extinguished at the Battle of Waterloo in 1815.

▲ Admiral Horatio Nelson (1758 – 1805), portrait from an engraving by R. Golding.

◄ *Opposite*: The east upper entrance, viewed from the bridge.

◄ Fort Nelson is named after the monument to Admiral Horatio Nelson, which has stood on this site since 1808. It predates the famous Nelson's Column in Trafalgar Square by over 30 years.

Fort Nelson through time

The story of Fort Nelson begins years before it was constructed and extends well beyond its decades of active service.

1805

During the Napoleonic Wars, the Royal Navy defeats the combined fleets of the French and Spanish Navies at the Battle of Trafalgar. Admiral Horatio Nelson is shot and killed during the battle.

1808

The Nelson Monument is completed atop Portsdown Hill overlooking Portsmouth – Britain's premier naval dockyard.

Decades of relative peace followed until 1848, when a new president of the French Second Republic was elected. His name was Louis-Napoleon Bonaparte, nephew of Emperor Napoleon I, a name to provoke a murmur of anxiety in British hearts. It was an anxiety that turned to alarm when he staged a startling coup d'état in 1851 and declared himself emperor, styling himself Napoleon III, a year later.

Ironically, however, when Britain found itself at war again in 1853, it was with France as an uneasy ally rather than an enemy. Together they fought alongside Turkey against the Russians in what became known as the Crimean War. Tellingly, one of its most famous engagements was the siege of Sebastopol, in which British, French and Turkish land forces subjected the home of Russia's fleet – the equivalent of Portsmouth in Britain – to a prolonged and eventually successful assault.

After the war, which ended in 1856, relations between Britain and France deteriorated. Tensions rose as Napoleon III presided over the strengthening of the Cherbourg naval base, sited almost directly across the Channel from Portsmouth. In language that reflected the antagonism between the two countries, British Prime Minister Lord Palmerston declared it to be 'a dagger pointed at the heart of this country'. Three years later, the French launched *La Gloire*, the world's first ocean-going iron-clad warship. As a result, when France flexed her military muscles in 1859 to support Italy in its war against the Austrian Empire, the prospect of her turning her eyes once more to the north seemed all too realistic.

In 1860 Palmerston organised a Royal Commission on the Defence of the United Kingdom, with a

▶ Portrait of Prime Minister Lord Palmerston (1784 – 1865), by Francis Cruikshank. © National Portrait Gallery, London

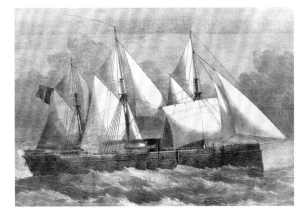

▼ 'The Iron-coated French Frigate La Gloire', *Illustrated London News*, 9 March 1861.

1815

The Napoleonic Wars come to an end with the defeat of the French forces led by Emperor Napoleon I at the Battle of Waterloo.

1848

Louis-Napoleon Bonaparte, nephew of Napoleon I, becomes president of the French Second Republic.

© United States Library of Congress

1852

Bonaparte declares himself Emperor Napoleon III of the Second French Empire, igniting fears of a renewed military threat to Britain.

particular focus on Portsmouth. Its findings reflected the Government's worst fears. Advances in artillery technology had rendered the existing defences around Britain's premier naval base and dockyard redundant. If Napoleon III were to land his forces elsewhere along the coast and occupy Portsdown Hill overlooking the city, the French could subject Portsmouth to just the kind of prolonged and lethal bombardment that had led to the fall of Sebastopol. Something had to be done, and quickly, and plans for what became known as the Palmerston Forts were set in motion. The idea of Fort Nelson was born.

"Any blow that may be launched from Cherbourg will be short, it will be straight, deadly and decisive, aimed at England's very heart." *The Times,* 13 July 1858

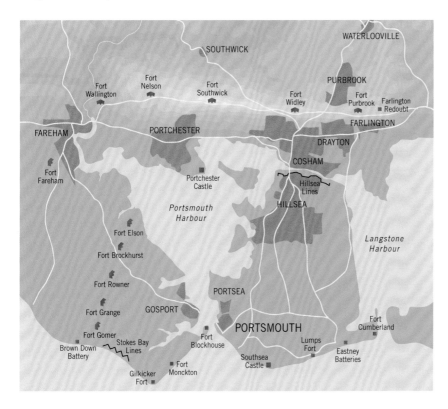

◄ This map shows the position of the forts designed to protect Portsmouth Harbour. The five new Palmerston Forts built on Portsdown Hill (Wallington, Nelson, Southwick, Widley and Purbrook) can be seen to the north of the harbour running in a line from west to east.

1853-56	1858	1859
Britain and France form an uneasy alliance to fight alongside Turkey against Russia in what becomes known as the Crimean War.	Napoleon III oversees improvements to the French naval port of Cherbourg, just a few hours steaming time from Portsmouth. British Prime Minister, Lord Palmerston, declares it to be 'a dagger pointed at the heart of this country'.	Prompted by public concern about the growing military and naval power of the French Empire, Lord Palmerston instigates an urgent Royal Commission on the Defence of the United Kingdom.

The Story of Fort Nelson

How was Fort Nelson built?

The Government's plan to defend Portsmouth involved building a line of forts along Portsdown Hill to deny enemy artillery access to the ridge overlooking the city. The guns of these forts would be trained inland to greet any attackers with ferocious overlapping fields of fire.

Once the decision to proceed with this plan was taken, work began with noticeable urgency. Protests that the building works would destroy an important natural recreational resource for local residents – 'our very lungs' as the *Portsmouth Times* put it – were ignored. The annual fair held on Portsdown Hill was summarily cancelled. Rather than let red tape get in the way, specialist surveyors from the Royal Engineers were told not to worry about causing any damage to crops growing on the affected land – angry tenant farmers were simply told to refer to the authorities for compensation. Indeed, deals to buy all the relevant land were agreed remarkably quickly.

▶ The polygonal shape of Fort Nelson can be seen clearly in this plan drawn in 1861 by the Royal Engineers. The proposed barracks building is semi-circular.

© The National Archives

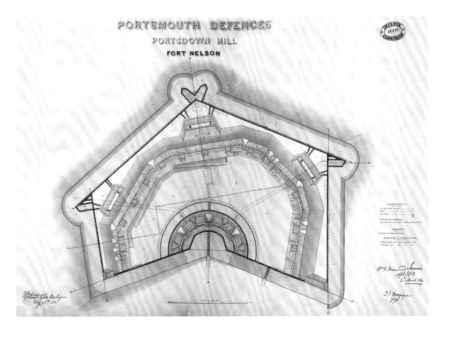

PORTSMOUTH DEFENCES
PORTSDOWN HILL
FORT NELSON

1860

The Royal Commission announces recommendations that include the building of a ring of forts on the hills surrounding Portsmouth to protect the naval base from attack.

1861

Work begins on the site of what will become Fort Nelson. It will continue for the next ten years.

Contracts to carry out the work were put out to tender and, in another sign of the Government's urgency, they were split into two parts: the first to create the earthworks – digging the ditches and throwing up the ramparts – to be completed in a matter of two to three months; the second to carry out the building work over a much longer period. This was to ensure that within three months of the work beginning, it would be possible in an emergency to mount guns in the earthworks.

So it was that in May 1861, teams of navvies began work on the site intended to become Fort Nelson. Garish white scars were torn in the rolling green of the hillside as the chalk beneath was revealed. The following year, with the dry ditch and earthen parapet in place, the building work began – all at a pace and cost that continued to speak volumes for the Government's priorities.

▲ Detail of flint work. The fort had to be protected against attack by strong walls built of excavated flint and locally made bricks.

▼ Some navvies worked in the Crimea, labouring for the British troops there. 'Navvies for the Crimea: the address to the navvies on board "The Hesperus", *Illustrated London News*, 13 January 1855.

▼ View from inside the west gate where original chalk blocks used in the construction of Fort Nelson are visible at the base of the wall.

Who designed and built Fort Nelson?

The contract to construct Fort Nelson – as well as two more of the Palmerston Forts – was won by William Tredwell, a civilian contractor whose experience of working on large railway projects with tight deadlines seems to have counted in his favour. He was also the lowest bidder, quoting £54,236 to complete the first stage of construction.

He worked to an overall design drawn up by William Crossman, a Royal Engineer under the Inspector General of Fortifications, and to detailed drawings prepared on site by other military and civilian surveyors as the project progressed.

The labour itself was carried out by hundreds of navvies – the workmen whose prowess with a pick, shovel and wheelbarrow lay behind the extraordinary array of railways, canals, reservoirs and sewers constructed during the Victorian era. So hardy and skilled were these navvies that they were reputed to shift some 20 tons of earth a day – enough to fill an average bath tub 60 times over – as well as to drink the same number of pints of beer. In fact, the construction process required so much surplus chalk to be shifted away from the site that it was decided to revise the original plans to reduce the burden. The solution? Raise the level of the fort's parade ground by five inches, so allowing for some 24,000 cubic yards of chalk to remain on site.

Drawing on his previous experience, Tredwell decided to construct railway lines – above and below ground – to link the three forts that he was building to Fareham, so that materials could be ferried to and from the sites more easily. Today, the precise locations of some of the tunnels that Tredwell constructed remain a mystery, including one shown close to Fort Nelson in this etching from *Illustrated Times*, 1863.

The Story of Fort Nelson

Who manned Fort Nelson?

One of the other recommendations of the Royal Commission set up by Lord Palmerston was that the small British Army, which was dangerously overextended guarding the British Empire, should be bolstered by raising volunteers.

Despite the fact that no wages were offered, this proved to be an extremely popular measure, with many men fired up by a sense of patriotic duty and the chance to serve in uniform alongside their friends and neighbours.

Many of the volunteers in the Portsmouth area were earmarked for service in the new Palmerston Forts, and in September 1871, two companies of the First Battalion of the Fourth Regiment of Foot marched in to Fort Nelson, made up of seven regular army officers, 171 volunteers, two horses, 17 wives and 24 children – listed in that order in the records.

▶ *Above right:* 'Wet Canteen' garrison members welcome visiting families at a fort, from a 19th century print.

▶ Scene of a hutted camp such as Aldershot. It is typical of a Victorian garrison's barracks.

1870

France declares war on Prussia. By early 1871, the French have been defeated, so removing the potential threat to Britain of Napoleon III.

1871

Work on Fort Nelson is completed and the first troops march in.

What was life like at Fort Nelson?

The accommodation awaiting these first volunteers comprised nine barrack rooms each providing space for around 20 men, although married soldiers and their families were also expected to share this accommodation with the single men.

Spartan though these rooms were, to soldiers from even just a generation earlier, they would have seemed luxurious. Gone were the days of overcrowded, poorly-ventilated barrack rooms where soldiers were, for example, expected to sleep two to a bed. This was in large part down to the campaigning work of Florence Nightingale, a pioneering nurse who had been appalled by the conditions endured by the men during the Crimean War, where many died not due to their wounds but to preventable diseases spread by poor sanitation.

On her return from the Crimea, Nightingale campaigned vigorously for radical changes in military healthcare and found a powerful ally in Prime Minister Lord Palmerston. It was no coincidence that the new forts destined to bear his name featured large airy barrack rooms, a ten-bed hospital, a dispensary and medical stores. You can see reconstructions of the barrack rooms and hospital at Fort Nelson today.

◀ The barrack rooms display at Fort Nelson.

1880s

The British Army engages in military manoeuvres to practise attacking and defending Portsmouth. In 1886, Fort Nelson finally receives its armament.

▶ The officers' mess kitchen, complete with working cooking range.

The food provided for the men was adequate but basic; most of it was boiled in the cookhouse and collected in bulk to be eaten in the barrack rooms, with the beds telescoped to the sides to make space. The non-commissioned officers, meanwhile, had a dining room known as a 'mess' on the first floor of the barracks, while the commissioned officers maintained the lifestyle of their class. Their quarters on the first floor were relatively luxurious, with a fine officers' mess and a drawing room looking out over the Solent. Indoor toilets were provided and rooms for the mess servants. You can see the restored officers' mess kitchen on the ground floor.

Washing facilities for the volunteers on the other hand were primitive, with cold water basins provided in an ablutions room accessible from the street outside the barracks. The lavatories, also reached from the street, were in an uncovered room, which must have been an unappealing prospect during the bitter cold of winter.

▼ The officers' mess on the first floor of the barracks.

▼ *Below right:* Ablutions room with slate sinks.

How was Fort Nelson first used?

B y the time the first volunteers marched into Fort Nelson, the threat that it had been built to counter was expiring. In 1871, the year of the fort's completion, France was defeated by a vigorous Prussia, intent on securing German unification. The enemy across the water had been vanquished.

But the uncomfortable truth was that even if the French had remained capable of mounting an attack on Portsmouth, the expensive new Palmerston Forts would have been powerless to stop them. In the decade since work had begun on the forts, there had been rapid advances in artillery so that any enemy attacking Portsmouth could do so from much greater distance, rendering Portsdown Hill of little strategic importance.

It is arguable whether such advances could have been predicted back in 1860, or whether the Government could or should have looked that far ahead given the perceived imminence of the threat from France at the time. Nonetheless, the forts quickly became known as 'Palmerston's Follies' and it was all too easy for the ill-founded rumour to take hold that they had been built facing the wrong way.

The War Office, having built the Palmerston Forts, felt obliged to make best use of them. The Inspector General of Fortifications even claimed in 1874 that they 'now secure the object for which they were designed'. This seems a relatively far-fetched claim given that Fort Nelson, for example, was not properly armed until 1886.

◀ A cast-iron smooth-bore 68-pounder gun in a restored embrasure facing inland over the North Caponier. AL.182.1

Fort Nelson and the First World War

By the mid-1880s it was already apparent that Germany, unified in 1871, was on its way to becoming the dominant military force on the continent. Over the course of the next few decades, the British Government found itself in an expensive arms race with its powerful new rival and was once more forced to carry out a drastic defence review. This eventually saw Fort Nelson stripped of its armament in 1903 and by 1911 it had become a training base for a battery of the newly formed Royal Garrison Artillery. A report by the Inspector of Garrison Artillery from around this time gives a good account of the drills that were carried out here, with the men learning to use the modern 60-pounder breech-loading gun, which was to prove an essential weapon during the First World War.

▶ *Above right:* The West Demi Caponier was used as an overflow barracks during the First World War.

▶ The 60-pounder BL gun of 5-inch calibre was the medium gun of the Royal Artillery from early in the 20th century.

1900s

After a review of Britain's defences in the light of a growing military threat from Germany, Fort Nelson's fixed armament is removed.

1913

Fort Nelson is re-equipped as a training base for a battery of the Royal Garrison Artillery.

1914-1918

During the First World War, Fort Nelson acts as a training and transit base for troops destined for the Western Front.

During the war itself, Fort Nelson became even busier, acting as a training camp and transit base for troops destined for the Western Front. All spaces, suitable or not, were hastily converted into accommodation – including the dank recesses of the empty mortar batteries and caponiers. It is hard not to sympathise with Private George Weston, who wrote from Fort Nelson in 1914:

'It's like being in an opening hole. The cliffs rise up above the grim old fort shutting out all sunshine but not the wind by any means.'

◀ Officer and NCOs of 108 Heavy Battery RGA, Fort Nelson, December 1913.

▼ This watercolour of Royal Garrison Artillery with a coast defence gun is dated 1910. It is by the military artist Richard Simkin (1850–1926). It shows gun crew dressed in 1902 khaki uniform. In the foreground, the officers and men are in full dress, based on the late Victorian uniform of the Royal Artillery. I.1289

A new war and a new role

The First World War saw aircraft begin to play a role over the battlefields, promising a revolution in the way that wars would be fought in years to come – and eventually leading to a new role for Fort Nelson. As early as 1924, British Government experts recognised that anti-aircraft defences would be crucial to keeping the enemy at bay in any future war. However, it was not until the late 1930s, when tensions with Germany reached breaking point, that work on these defences really started.

Close to 60 anti-aircraft batteries were set up along the coastline around Southampton and Portsmouth – the highest concentration of such defences outside London. Most were equipped with 3.7-inch 'Ack-Ack' guns and the excellent Swedish Bofors 40-mm automatic gun for close defence.

▼ A 3.7-inch anti-aircraft gun and a Swedish Bofors 40-mm automatic gun (*right*) in the Voice of the Guns gallery.
Bofors image © Jonty Wilde

1938

Fort Nelson is fitted out to become a major ammunition store, intended to supply anti-aircraft batteries around Portsmouth and Southampton.

In 1938, work began to convert Fort Nelson into an ammunition depot to supply all of these batteries. Ten brick and concrete magazines were built on the Parade, two of which can still be seen today. Together they were capable of holding 42,000 rounds of 3.7-inch and 5.25-inch ammunition, with thousands more 40-mm rounds stored in the fort's underground magazine. It was at this time that a conveyor belt was added to the main tunnel, and a narrow-gauge railway laid along the street, to make the handling of ammunition more efficient.

▲ Fort Nelson from the air in the spring of 1988. Five of the ten Second World War anti-aircraft magazines are visible on the Parade.

◄ View of the street showing the narrow-gauge railtrack running alongside the tunnel entrances.

1940

As the Battle of Britain rages through the summer months, and the Blitz begins in September, Fort Nelson is pressed into sustained action.

1941

On the night of 9-10 January, during a raid on Portsmouth, German aircraft drop several bombs on the area around Fort Nelson. The fort is commended for carrying out its dangerous duties regardless.

1945

After the war, the fort becomes a storage area for military equipment, but is gradually allowed to deteriorate.

West gates and Guardroom

▶ View from the new west gate built during the Second World War.

The Parade perimeter was concreted and a new west gate built to allow lorries to enter the fort on one side and follow a one-way system to exit on the other. If this part of the fort's transformation was immediately obvious, others were more subtle; foliage was allowed to grow over the ramparts to provide camouflage, and openings to the fort were bricked up to deter possible saboteurs.

Operating the ammunition depot was inherently dangerous work for the Royal Army Ordnance Corps whose job it was to handle the ammunition, as well as for the occupying infantry. This was never more the case than on the night of 9-10 January 1941 when the fort was rocked by a heavy raid. Despite the fact that a direct hit to the magazines could have torn the whole hillside apart, the men stuck to their task, earning themselves a commendation for their:

'unstinting efforts in supplying a further 1,220 rounds of ammunition by night to the various gun positions'.

▶ Bricked up gun ports in the West Demi Caponier.

▶ *Right:* The narrow-gauge railtrack leading to the original west gate. To the right is the entrance to the guardroom and cells.

Reminders of this period of Fort Nelson's history can still be seen today. In the Voice of the Guns gallery, you can see a 3.7-inch anti-aircraft gun of the type that the fort kept supplied, and in the guardroom close to the west gate you can examine the many examples of graffiti that the men drew on the walls in their more idle moments, including a graphic depiction of a Bren gun pointing directly at Hitler's head.

▲ An example of the graffiti in the guardroom.

▼ A view of the graffiti-covered walls inside the guardroom.

Saved for the nation

▲ The west entrance and barracks before restoration, April 1980.

▶ Aerial view of Fort Nelson in 2007.

After the Second World War, Fort Nelson was used for the storage of vast amounts of military equipment and later became a naval depot. But some areas were allowed to deteriorate and eventually, with defence rationalisation, the fort was emptied, locked up and rarely entered.

Derelict and deserted, Fort Nelson might have gradually disappeared under the slow but relentless assault of nature, were it not for the intervention of Hampshire County Council, which bought the site from the Ministry of Defence in 1979. Work then began to restore the fort so that it could be put to some use, and by 1984 it was deemed fit to be opened to the public at weekends.

Given that the fort had originally been built to mount and resist artillery, attempts were made to find guns to put on display. This brought the site to the attention of the Royal Armouries, at a time when it was seeking suitable

1971

Despite falling into disrepair, Fort Nelson is designated as a Grade I Listed Building, in recognition of its unique historical and architectural significance.

1979

The site is bought from the Ministry of Defence by Hampshire County Council. Work begins on its restoration.

1984

Fort Nelson is opened to the public at weekends.

1988

The Royal Armouries leases Fort Nelson from Hampshire County Council, redoubling efforts to restore the site to its former glory.

locations to display some of its collection outside the Tower of London. The potential of the site was obvious: it was a classic artillery fortification with space not only to exhibit a range of guns, but to show Victorian heavy guns correctly emplaced, and even to hold demonstrations of the guns being fired.

Negotiations began and in 1988 the Royal Armouries was able to lease Fort Nelson from Hampshire County Council. The site was still far from fully restored, but thanks to the continuing work of specialist contractors, a Youth Training Scheme and dedicated volunteers from the Palmerston Forts Society – all supported by grants from English Heritage – it was finally opened as both an artillery museum and historic monument in 1995. Since then, the collection has continued to grow, as have visitor numbers, with hundreds of thousands of people flocking to the site.

▲ The west entrance to Fort Nelson after restoration.

▼ Members of the Portsdown Artillery Volunteers with the 64-pounder Palliser Rifled Muzzle-Loading gun. XIX.253

▼ The Voice of the Guns gallery.

1995

Fort Nelson is opened to the public not only as an historic monument but as home to the national collection of artillery.

2011

A new multi-million pound redevelopment programme results in new facilities including interactive galleries, a café and a visitor centre.

2016

Fort Nelson marks the 75th anniversary of the night it was targeted by German bombers during the Second World War.

2018

Fort Nelson hosts Poppies: *Wave*, from the installation 'Blood Swept Lands and Seas of Red', as part of events organised by 14-18 NOW.

FIRING THE GUNS

One of the great attractions of visiting the Royal Armouries at Fort Nelson is the chance to see one of the big guns being fired. It is a visceral reminder of the raw power of artillery that binds the fort and all of its exhibits together.

13-inch mortar firing in the North Mortar Battery.

A thrilling experience

Fort Nelson is one of the few places in Britain where you can experience live firings of historic artillery pieces. Two rounds are fired from one of the museum's big guns on the Parade. It is well worth taking up position a few minutes early to watch the preparations as well as the firing, which is carried out by specially trained members of Royal Armouries staff. You may also want to don one of our pairs of protective headphones to take the edge off the concussive roar of the gun.

The gun most often fired on the Parade is a 25-pounder Quick-Firing Gun Howitzer, of the type used extensively by the British Army during the Second World War. © Jonty Wilde

Echoes of Fort Nelson's Victorian heritage

On selected Sundays and at special events you can watch gun drills and firings carried out by uniformed detachments of the Portsdown Artillery Volunteers. Wearing the uniforms that would have been worn by the part-time Victorian soldiers who formed the fort's original garrison, these volunteers can also be seen having a meal in the barrack room or showing visitors around the underground magazine.

The volunteers specialise in firing the guns that were originally intended to form Fort Nelson's main armament. These include the 64-pounder guns and the 7-inch Armstrong rifled breech-loading gun on the ramparts, the 32-pounder smooth-bore breech-loading gun in the North Caponier, and a 13-inch mortar in the North Mortar Battery. It is fascinating to watch the finely tuned movements and timings required to put these big guns into action.

In addition you may also witness them firing the Victorian 16-pounder field gun, sometimes drawn into position by horses.

▲ Portsdown Artillery Volunteers firing a 64-pounder gun.

Working artillery from across the ages

On certain occasions throughout the year, you can see visiting enthusiasts demonstrating other forms of artillery, from the time before gunpowder was invented all the way through to pieces from the Second World War and beyond. To find out more about our calendar of events, visit www.royalarmouries.org

Enduring power

Fort Nelson is a place where you are invited not just to witness the guns being fired but to gain a healthy respect for their power. As you explore the fort, you will notice that a section of the Parade and ramparts is closed to visitors. This is to keep you a safe distance away from the area where the guns are fired each day, and from the explosive materials that are required for the demonstrations.

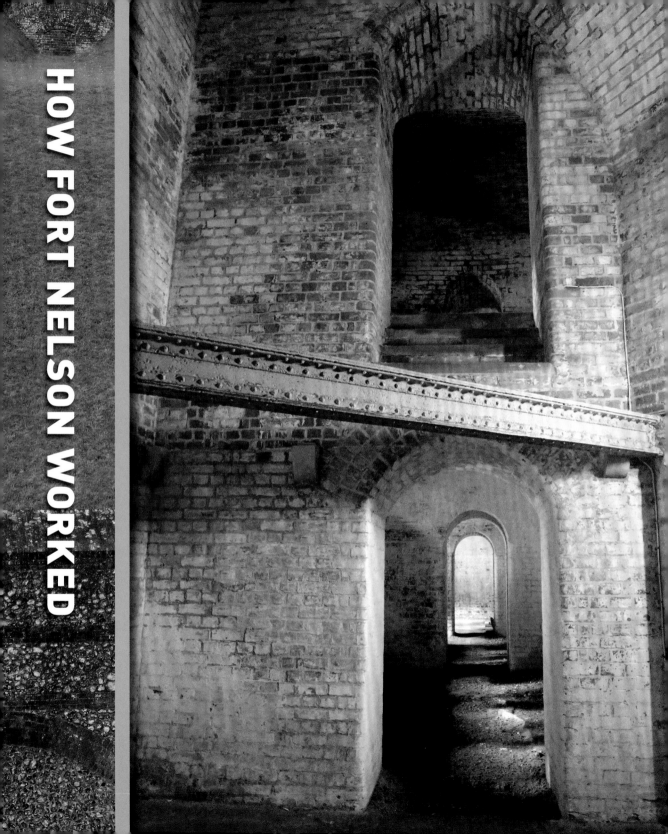

Fort Nelson was built according to contemporary military thinking but for a role that eventually proved unnecessary. Take a walk along its interlocking network of tunnels, gun emplacements and ramparts and you can begin to see just how difficult it would have been to overcome.

Fort Nelson was built for a war that never came and for a defensive purpose that was of little tactical use by the time construction was complete. Britain's military planners had simply not foreseen the astonishing revolution in artillery design that meant that enemy forces could launch a bombardment of Portsmouth from further away. It was no longer necessary to take Portsdown Hill first.

This would have been an enormous relief to any enemy force because the task of breaching the defences of Fort Nelson and the other Palmerston Forts would otherwise have been a fearsome prospect. Compact and dug down into the ground almost out of sight along the ridge, the forts gave enemy troops little at which to aim their guns, with the sloping face of the hillside serving to absorb or deflect shot and shell. As enemy troops probed for weaknesses between the forts, they would have been subjected to overlapping fields of fire so dense that no significant force would have been able to slip through.

◄ *Opposite:* Interior view of the North Caponier flanking gallery.

▼ Aerial view of Fort Nelson, 2017. © Aerial Photography Services

Street

Exploring the fort's defences

To get a sense of how Fort Nelson would have worked in action, take a walk along the street running along the length of the barracks. In peacetime this would simply have been a way for the men to reach everyday facilities such as the toilets or ablutions room, or to make their way out on to the Parade for drill practice. But during an attack it would have presented a very different scene.

As shells rained down overhead, the reason for the street's trench-like design would have become obvious, providing protection for the men as they went about their duties. Along the street itself, there would have been men and horses hauling carts and barrows of ammunition to supply the main guns on the ramparts. During the Second World War, a narrow-gauge railtrack was added to make the flow of ammunition easier – this time to load up the lorries waiting to carry it out to anti-aircraft batteries up and down the coast. You can still see this railtrack today, together with a replica ammunition wagon.

▶ The street, railtrack and replica ammunition wagon.

▼ Powder barrels in the underground magazine.

Going underground

As you walk along the street, you will notice entrances to three tunnels, each of which drops gradually away below ground – one close to each end of the street, and another 'main tunnel' part-way along. This network of tunnels was designed to give the men access to the two powder magazines buried deep below ground level, to three caponiers – North, East and West – where the fort's defences were most heavily concentrated, and to the three Mortar batteries. Today you can explore the main tunnel as part of your visit.

As you head down into the gloomy passageway, spare a thought for the men stationed here in Victorian times, who did not have the luxury of electricity, but instead had to rely on the flicker of candlelight. This, of course, presented a major problem, since it would have been catastrophic to expose the combustible materials stored in the powder magazines to a naked flame. For this reason, a separate lighting passage was constructed parallel to the main tunnel. Candle lamps were then lit outside, carried down this passage and positioned in small glass apertures, from where they could only cast a dim light into the underground passageways and rooms.

As you walk down the main tunnel, you will come across another precaution against explosion – a bypass tunnel that allowed men to get across the fort without going through the magazine itself. This was to stop the men's metal-studded boots creating any sparks as they hurried about their duties. You will also notice a conveyor belt running along the side of the tunnel. This was added during the Second World War to speed up the movement of Bofors ammunition to and from the magazine.

Tunnels

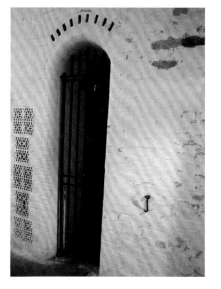

◀ *Left:* The entrance to the lighting passage.

◀ A view into the bypass tunnel.

Working in a magazine in any era is a hazardous business, but it must have been especially hard in Victorian times when all of the explosive materials had to be handled, measured, weighed and transported in the dimmest of light. Being on duty here during an attack must have been even more nerve-wracking – an experience that the Victorian volunteers did not ever have to go through, but which was endured during the Second World War when Portsmouth was bombed by the German Luftwaffe.

Much of the ammunition from the magazines would have been hauled up the tunnel to the street and from there to the big guns on the ramparts, or to the separate tunnels leading to the West or East Caponiers. But some would have been taken further along the main tunnel to supply the North Mortar Battery and North Caponier – a route that you can still follow today. It is only when you reach these outer defences that the full might of Fort Nelson starts to become even clearer.

▲ Weighing scales and shells.

▶ The conveyor belt in the central tunnel. This view is looking towards the street.

Outer defences

To take Fort Nelson, enemy troops would have to make their way up the sloping open fields outside the fort. When they came within two miles of the fort, they would have come under the fire of the heavy long-range guns of the main armament – situated up on the ramparts. This would have been hard enough to get past, but if they managed to do so, the men of Fort Nelson would have had plenty more defensive power to draw on.

As you make your way along the main tunnel, you will come across stairs leading up to the North Mortar Battery, sunk deep below ground level in a vaulted chamber designed to house three 13-inch cast-iron mortars. These would have been used to bring explosive shells raining down almost vertically on the enemy's siege works and his advance as he struggled up the nearby hillside.

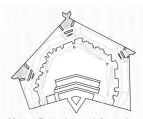

Mortar Batteries and Caponiers

◀ The cast-iron 13-inch mortar was near the end of its service life when Fort Nelson was prepared to receive nine of them in three protected batteries. Cumbersome to serve, the 13-inch mortar was nevertheless capable of throwing a heavy explosive bomb to about 2,700 yards with surprising accuracy. One of the Fort's 13-inch mortars is seen here being blank-fired by members of the Portsdown Artillery Volunteers. XIX.228

Today, you can see three such mortars as they would have been positioned in Victorian times – authentic examples of the artillery designed for use in the fort. When you examine their squat muscular barrels up close – and the round bombs that they were designed to fire – it is easy to imagine just how effective they would have been in defence of the fort. It is easier still if you visit on one of the special occasions when one of these carefully conserved mortars is fired by the Portsdown Artillery Volunteers (see pages 70-71).

Assuming that enemy troops were able to withstand the barrage of mortar fire, they would next have come to the deep dry ditch surrounding the high walls of the fort. They would now have been faced with a choice: attempt the major engineering feat of bridging the ditch; or lay explosives to collapse the edges of the ditch and so fill it in.

▲ Close-up of a gun in the North Caponier.

▶ *Above right:* The North Mortar Battery with 13-inch mortars.

▶ Looking along the dry ditch to the West Demi Caponier.

▶ *Opposite:* Lower floor of the North Caponier east gun gallery, with 32-pounder SBBL guns in place.

Whichever choice they made, they faced annihilation by the fire from guns hidden in the three caponiers, which projected out from the main body of the fort but below the level of the surrounding land.

Head further down the main tunnel and you can see the North Caponier for yourself. Here you will find four 32-pounder smooth-bore breech-loading (SBBL) guns on the two floors of the caponier, one of which can still be fired today by the Portsdown Artillery Volunteers. Look along their sleek barrels and you can see how these guns are trained to fire 'case shot' along the length of the dry ditch so that no attacker could approach the fort walls with impunity. Case shot was so called because it consisted of a hollow tubular 'case' of thin iron filled with lead balls. When fired, the case was designed to split open and release the balls so sending a deadly cloud of projectiles hurtling at enemy troops. Originally the North Caponier was designed to mount eight guns, with the two other demi-caponiers mounting four each.

▲ Members of the Portsdown Artillery Volunteers firing one of the 32-pounder SBBL guns in the North Caponier.

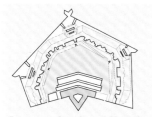

Ramparts, Parade and Barracks

Inner defences

Head back from the outer reaches of the North Caponier and climb the stairs to the North Mortar Battery, and you can follow a passageway that opens out onto the Parade, where more pieces from the Royal Armouries collection are on display, including some especially ornate guns from East Asia.

To the left and right, you can find sloping pathways that take you up onto the fort's ramparts. These pathways were part of the fort's original design, to allow armament and ammunition to be hauled up from the Parade.

It is on the ramparts that Fort Nelson's biggest guns were situated (see pages 44-45) but this part of the fortification also served another defensive purpose. In the unlikely event that the ditch defences failed and the enemy breached the outer walls of the fort, the inner loop-holed walls of the ramparts could serve as the next obstacle, through which the men of the garrison could lay down small-arms fire.

▶ Muzzle of an ornate Turkish 18-pounder gun, dated 1708. (This gun is in the display pictured below, third in the row.) XIX.115

▼ Display of East Asian guns on the Parade. In the foreground is an Indian 24-pounder gun, the muzzle and trunnion ends are formed as tiger's heads. XIX.99

As a last resort, the fort's defenders could fall back across the Parade to the barrack block, from where they could use their rifles at the embrasures and employ the cannon placed on the roof. If an enemy reached this far, of course, the garrison would have failed to hold their part of Portsdown Hill and they would no longer have been able to mount an effective defence of Portsmouth. But any enemy that achieved such a feat of arms would undoubtedly have done so at great cost.

▲ *Above left:* View over the West Demi-Caponier. © Jonty Wilde

▲ *Above:* Flanking gallery, North Caponier.

▼ The Parade and Artillery Hall viewed from the ramparts near the west gate. © Jonty Wilde

Ramparts and big guns

Fort Nelson's big guns

The guns that you can see on the ramparts of Fort Nelson today illustrate the rapid advances in artillery technology that took place whilst the fort was being constructed. Originally the plan was to arm the fort entirely with cast-iron smooth-bore weapons – 13-inch mortars and 32-pounders for the outer defences and massive 68-pounders on the ramparts.

An example of one of these 68-pounders can be seen mounted in one of the restored embrasures today, but only to illustrate the original plans for the fort. In reality, by the time that Fort Nelson had been constructed, smooth-bore guns of this kind were fast becoming obsolete. A revolution in artillery design had seen the introduction of new rifled guns, which had much greater range and accuracy (see pages 60-61).

Two examples of rifled guns can be seen on the ramparts today, similar to ones known to have been part of Fort Nelson's armament in 1893. The first is a 64-pounder Palliser rifled muzzle-loading gun, which was made by converting a smooth-bore weapon 8 inches in calibre. Many obsolete smooth-bore guns were made use of in this way, by inserting a rifled wrought-iron tube into a suitably re-bored gun. That way the old gun could still be used with its old mounting but to much greater effect. The example at Fort Nelson

▲ Weighing nearly 5 tons, the cast-iron smooth-bore 68-pounder was mainly intended for use with the Royal Navy. In fact you can see the same kind of guns on HMS *Warrior* – an armoured battleship launched in 1860, now a museum ship in Portsmouth Dockyard. AL.182.1

▶ 64-pounder Palliser rifled muzzle-loading gun. XIX.253
© Jonty Wilde

is mounted on a replica elevated carriage, designed so that the gun could fire over a high parapet. It is still fired on special occasions today.

The second is a light 110-pounder (7-inch) Armstrong rifled breech-loading gun – the only surviving example of its type – which has been restored to firing condition by the Royal Armouries and mounted on a replica carriage. It is located in what is known as the West 'Haxo Casemate', a type of defensive structure named after the French military engineer who first devised it – François-Nicolas-Benoît Haxo, one of Napoleon I's most trusted generals. The casemate is a vaulted chamber built on top of the gun platform to protect the gun and its detachment from enemy fire.

▲ *Above left:* Exterior of the West 'Haxo Casemate'.

▲ *Above:* Drill carried out by a gun detachment of Portsdown Artillery Volunteers.

◀ The 110-pounder (7-inch) Armstrong rifled breech-loading gun inside the casemate. XIX.506

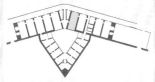

Art of Artillery

ARMS AND ART

One of the galleries in the barracks building houses an exhibition called the Art of Artillery, where you can see some of the most extraordinary guns in the Royal Armouries collection – guns designed for show as well as for shooting.

Guns as status symbols

▼ This extraordinary piece was commissioned by the Commander of the Artillery of the Order of St John of Malta for its Grand Master. Its carriage is carved with depictions of the Furies – the avenging female figures of Greek mythology – which has led to the piece being called the Furies gun. It is thought to date from 1773. XIX.79

The relationship between artillery and art stretches back to when guns first appeared on the battlefield. Their brutal destructive power inspired such awe that they were celebrated as 'Gods of War', with some pieces lavished with decoration to pay tribute to their status.

It was a status shared by those who could boast such weapons in their armoury, not only because of the military power inherent in their use but also because of the political authority that they therefore conferred and the undeniable proof they provided of the owner's wealth.

The importance of bronze

Many early guns were constructed from wrought iron, which gave little scope for decoration. However, the use of bronze, which is well suited to being cast, gave gun-founders from the fifteenth to the nineteenth century plenty of opportunity to apply ornament to what we might consider to be brutal weapons of destruction. It is little wonder that they were expected to make full use of this ability. Making such guns involved expensive materials and processes, so whoever had the money to commission such work expected to see a result that looked the part.

▶ This French Bronze Robinet cannon was brought to England after the Battle of Waterloo in 1815. Adorned with relief castings of peasant figures, reptilian wyverns and a winged mermaid, it is a particularly slender and elegant piece which dates from 1535. XIX.166

Showpieces, gifts and trophies

Many decorative guns were not intended for use in earnest. They were showpieces for their owners or designed as gifts to forge diplomatic ties and strengthen alliances. Whatever their provenance, the most handsome guns also made fitting trophies for triumphant kings, princes and generals to be displayed as objects of national pride to visiting dignitaries. The Royal Armouries at the Tower of London, though originally set up to perform a military role, gradually came to act as a showcase for this country – a showcase now partly housed at Fort Nelson.

◀ This beautifully cast barrel is in the form of a dragon, matching the destructive power of the gun to the fire-breathing fury of the mythical beast. Thought to date from the late eighteenth century, it is one of four similar guns taken from the palace of King Thebaw at Mandalay in Burma after the British victory over the Burmese in 1885. XIX.123

Today Fort Nelson is home to the artillery collection of the Royal Armouries, with visitors able to see hundreds of big guns from around the world and across the centuries. The best place to get a sense of the collection's scope is to start in the Voice of the Guns gallery – the first gallery you come to when entering the fort.

Voice of the Guns

The two-storey Voice of the Guns gallery contains some of the most remarkable guns from the Middle Ages to the late twentieth century. Two of the most dramatic pieces confront you as you enter: the bronze Great Turkish Bombard of 1464 with its beautiful calligraphic muzzle, and the gleaming Sheffield steel of two 'Supergun' tubes, part of the monster gun commissioned by Saddam Hussein in the 1980s and seized by British Customs before they were shipped.

If you head down the stairs from the entrance level, you will also see key examples of artillery, each with its own story to tell. Particularly impressive are the rival German and British anti-aircraft guns of the Second World War: the legendary German '88' and the British 3.7-inch, famous for its role during the Blitz. It was in keeping the latter supplied with ammunition that Fort Nelson earned itself a commendation during the Second World War.

◀ *Opposite:* The German '88' and British 3.7-inch anti-aircraft guns in the Voice of the Guns gallery. XIX.331 and XIX.840

◀ The entrance level of the Voice of the Guns gallery. © Jonty Wilde

Artillery Hall

The Artillery Hall

I f you exit the Voice of the Guns gallery from its upper level, you can make your way forward to the magnificent Artillery Hall, pausing along the way to see a British 4.5-inch AA gun and a pair of fine bronze English cannon made from French guns captured at Cherbourg in 1757.

▶ A British 4.5-inch AA naval gun on the Parade. XIX.954

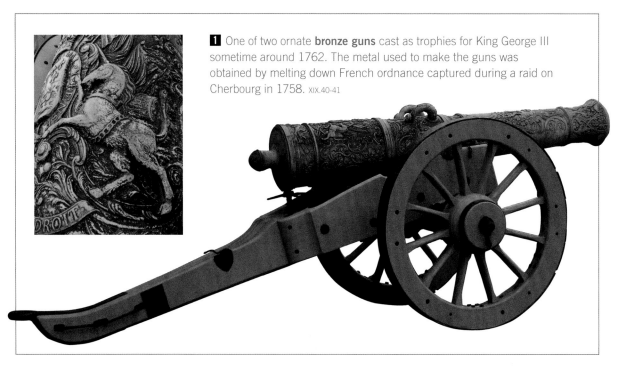

1 One of two ornate **bronze guns** cast as trophies for King George III sometime around 1762. The metal used to make the guns was obtained by melting down French ordnance captured during a raid on Cherbourg in 1758. XIX.40-41

THE ROYAL ARMOURIES COLLECTION **51**

In the Artillery Hall itself, you can see the main conservation workshop and some of the finest early bronze guns leading on to the heavy guns of the eighteenth and nineteenth centuries. Then, in the vast Twentieth Century Gallery, there are examples of some of the main weapons from the First World War, Second World War, Cold War and beyond.

Amongst many iconic and rare weapons, it is worth looking out for the German 'squeeze-bore' 75/55-mm Pak 41 anti-tank gun (see page 66) and the Gerald Bull-designed long-range 155-mm howitzer (see page 69).

◄ A view inside Artillery Hall. In the foreground is an 18-pounder Quick-Firing Field Gun. XIX.529 © Jonty Wilde

Conservation of artillery

Caring for the national collection of artillery is fundamental to the work of the Royal Armouries at Fort Nelson. It is a responsibility that falls to a staff of conservation specialists, supported by a team of valued volunteers.

Naturally their work centres on the preservation of guns – some of which are several centuries old – but it also extends to related artillery equipment such as projectiles, mortar beds and carriages. Whatever the purpose of the object, what matters most to the conservator is the material from which it is made, which can vary from all kinds of metal to wood, leather, rubber, plastic, paper and paintwork. It is the material that dictates the most appropriate method of treatment – whether it be a tried and tested technique common to many areas of conservation, or a new and potentially better method pioneered by our team of experts.

We have a laboratory and workshops dedicated to conservation at Fort Nelson, and you can often see our larger guns being worked on at the east end of the Artillery Hall. Many visitors are particularly interested to see the special immersion tanks located here, which are designed to counter the corrosive effects of salt water on guns recovered from the sea bed. We also hold regular talks on conservation which are advertised in our events programme

The regular gun-firing displays could also not happen without the work of the conservation team, who make sure that all of our firing guns are in good working order, and prepare all the necessary ammunition.

▲ A 17th-century gun recovered from the wreck of the Royal Navy ship HMS *London* in the conservation tank.

The Story of Artillery

The Story of Artillery

Housed inside the Barracks building is a series of galleries telling the chronological Story of Artillery. Here you can gain an appreciation of how these weapons have evolved over the centuries, with key pieces exhibited along the way. It is a story worth telling in more detail over the coming pages, drawing on the many other guns that you can discover in the grounds of the fort, in the Voice of the Guns gallery and in the Artillery Hall.

Fighting at a distance

The word 'artillery' describes weapons that share two chief characteristics: firstly that they are capable of projecting missiles that are too heavy or dangerous to throw by hand; secondly that the weapons themselves are too weighty to be carried and used by one person.

The earliest artillery weapons relied on the spring power of a bow and bowstring – using the same principle as a hand-bow but at a scale that required mechanical assistance to be operated. To gain increased power the Ancient Greeks introduced the catapult, which retained the bowstring but replaced the bow with vertical torsion springs. Two arms connected by the

▶ Illustration of a 4th-century AD Roman stone-throwing catapult. It was sometimes called an *onager*, the Latin word for a wild ass.

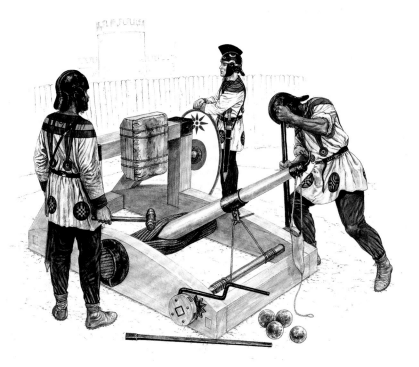

bowstring were each fitted into the springs, which were made of hair or sinew and housed vertically in a strong frame. Such artillery was built either to shoot heavy arrows or spherical stone projectiles.

These Greek designs were copied and improved by the Romans, which made really large machines possible. They proved to be so effective that they were still being built during the Middle Ages, but medieval artillery engineers also created a new machine – the trebuchet – which probably originated in the Levant in the 12th century. Operating on a completely different principle, the trebuchet consisted of a long vertical arm, one end fitted with a sling that carried the projectile, and the other with a heavy counterweight. To shoot, the arm was winched down so that the counterweight was raised. This was then allowed to drop, so lifting the other end of the arm and launching the projectile. You can see working replicas of these mechanical artillery weapons in the Artillery Hall, some of which are demonstrated from time to time.

▲ 15th-century depiction of a counterweight trebuchet. From *Alte Armatur und Ringkunst* (Fechtbuch) 1459, Thalhofer [Talhoffer], Hans, Thott 290 folio.
© Royal Danish Library

Gunpowder and guns

At around the same time as the trebuchet was first used, the evolution of artillery went through a dramatic step-change with the invention of the 'firearm'. This development was based on the use of gunpowder, which was first made in China for the gentler – though noisy – purposes of fireworks.

The first dated picture of a firearm in the West is the now famous arrow-shooting weapon illustrated in *The Duty of Kings*, a book written for the future King Edward III in 1326 by Walter de Milemete. The drawing shows a vase-shaped device, supported by trestles. The gunner is using a red-hot rod to ignite the charge to fire a large arrow. A contemporary account describes a test of the weapon in which the arrow flew so far that it killed an unsuspecting workman, so, while uncertainty remains over the exact details of the nature, scale and proportions of the gun, there is no doubt that such weapons existed at this time, and could be effective.

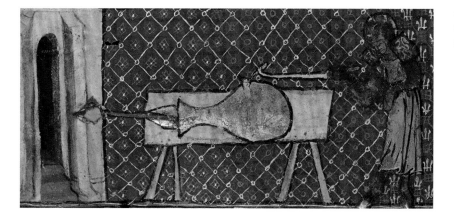

◀ Detail from *The Duty of Kings*. Christ Church MS 92 folio 70v.
© Christ Church Library

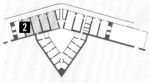

The Story of Artillery

Age of the bombard

The gun described by Walter de Milemete was cast in bronze, which involved heating the metal into its liquid form and then pouring it into a mould. However, the constituent metals of bronze – copper and tin – were expensive and relatively difficult to come by, so as early gun-makers took on the challenge of making ever larger guns, they turned to iron as an alternative. This meant relying on a different method of manufacture because, until the mid-sixteenth century, it was impossible to build an effective gun out of cast iron. Instead craftsmen made use of wrought iron, using the well-tried arts of the blacksmith to shape the heated metal by hammer.

They would first forge a chamber to house the gunpowder, and then build a wider tube through which the projectile would be fired. This was built up of long bars bound together by wrought iron hoops – in much the same way that a wooden barrel is built. It is no coincidence, then, that this tube came to be known as the gun's barrel.

▲ Illustration of a 15th-century wrought-iron bombard similar to the Boxted Bombard. The bombard and its crew were protected from enemy fire by a pivoting timber shield.

2 The wrought-iron **Boxted Bombard** is named after Boxted Hall in Suffolk, outside which it had stood for some two hundred years before being acquired by the Royal Armouries in the 1980s. It is thought to have been manufactured in Sussex around 1450. XIX.314

It was by using these methods that fourteenth-century craftsmen created the siege bombard, designed to hurl a massive stone ball at the walls of castles and cities. The use of these wall-smashers contributed to the fall of Constantinople, capital of the Byzantine Empire and the strongest city in Christendom, to the Ottoman Turks after a long siege in 1453. After this shattering event, it was impossible to deny the power of gunpowder.

Voice of the Guns

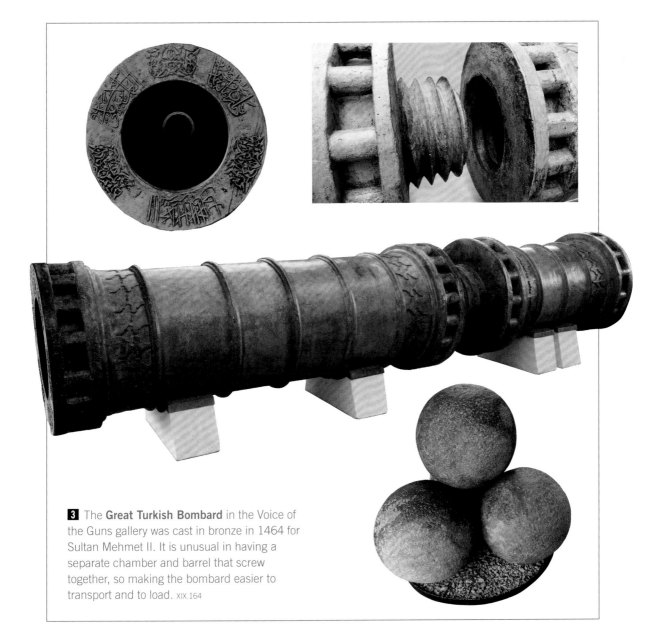

3 The **Great Turkish Bombard** in the Voice of the Guns gallery was cast in bronze in 1464 for Sultan Mehmet II. It is unusual in having a separate chamber and barrel that screw together, so making the bombard easier to transport and to load. XIX.164

The Story of Artillery

Iron bound or bronze cast

The drawback of bombards was that they were expensive and laborious to produce, difficult to move, had to be positioned close to the target to have a significant effect, and needed to be guarded from enemy assault. This led to the manufacture of wrought-iron guns of much smaller calibre, which could therefore be deployed more easily on the battlefield and on ships.

These guns were loaded at the breech at the base of the gun, making use of a separate powder chamber that was wedged into place after the projectile had been loaded into the barrel. Two or three chambers were supplied to allow a high rate of fire. The larger guns of this type fired stone shot or anti-personnel ammunition consisting of stone fragments in a wooden container; the smaller guns could fire lead or composite shot. The invention of wheeled gun carriages in the 1450s meant that these guns could be used in a more versatile way, and some were mounted on a pivot to make them even better suited for anti-personnel use.

One danger with wrought-iron guns, especially the breech-loading type, was that the joins between chamber and barrel, or between the component sections of the barrel, made it more likely that the gun could split when fired. This not only endangered the gunners but rendered the gun useless until repaired.

Guns cast in one piece from bronze – and loaded via the muzzle – were safer in this respect, but were slower to load and much more expensive to produce. As is so often the case, the solution to this problem, when it was arrived at in the mid-sixteenth century, was driven by military need. King Henry VIII, having made powerful enemies abroad by divorcing Katharine of Aragon,

▶ *Opposite:* Portrait of Henry VIII, after Hans Holbein the Younger, late 16th century. I.51

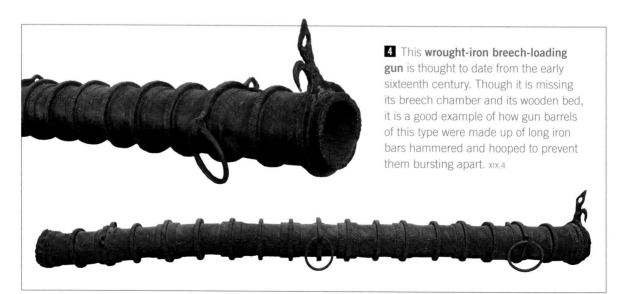

4 This **wrought-iron breech-loading gun** is thought to date from the early sixteenth century. Though it is missing its breech chamber and its wooden bed, it is a good example of how gun barrels of this type were made up of long iron bars hammered and hooped to prevent them bursting apart. XIX.4

needed to arm his fleet, army and coastal fortifications, but did not have the funds to bankroll his grand designs. What he did have, however, was the expertise of foreign craftsmen, and access to a supply of quality English iron ore.

Under Henry's patronage, Peter Baude, a French gun-founding expert, and Ralph Hogge discovered a way to cast large guns in iron – a much cheaper metal than bronze. Soon, English iron guns were renowned far and wide, and so successful were they that cast-iron muzzle-loading weapons of this type were used almost exclusively until the mid-nineteenth century – becoming the preferred armament for English ships, coastal forts and siege artillery.

There was still a demand for cast bronze guns during this period, especially when it came to field guns, which needed to be lighter. Bronze was preferred by naval gun crews since the softer metal gave warning of an impending burst by bulging outwards (more brittle cast iron merely fractured – with fatal consequences). It was also easier to adorn with decorative touches and had a distinctive handsome sheen.

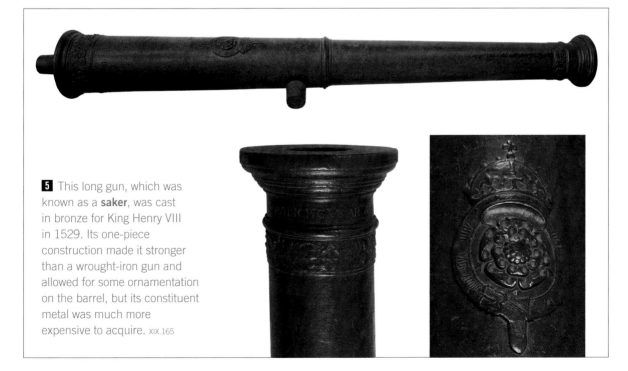

5 This long gun, which was known as a **saker**, was cast in bronze for King Henry VIII in 1529. Its one-piece construction made it stronger than a wrought-iron gun and allowed for some ornamentation on the barrel, but its constituent metal was much more expensive to acquire. XIX.165

Artillery Hall

Three centuries of evolution

Although cast, muzzle-loading guns dominated the battlefield on land and sea for almost three hundred years, they were not capable of great accuracy or great efficiency when it came to the ratio between their weight of shot and their range. In battle, other factors tended to be crucial – such as the availability of guns, ammunition and trained gunners, or the way the guns were used. Mobility on land remained a challenge, for example, so in 1759 Frederick the Great of Prussia pioneered the use of Horse Artillery – light guns that, with their gunners, were able to keep up with cavalry.

One development which did lead to an improvement in gun design came at the beginning of the eighteenth century. Until that time, guns were cast by pouring molten metal into a tubular mould so that the barrel solidified with a ready-made bore. The inner surface of the bore would then be machined to give it a good smooth finish. Then Jean Maritz, the son of an expert lathe

▼ Illustration of the wreck of the *Royal George*. Fresh Water and Marine Image Bank, University of Washington

6 This **bronze 24-pounder naval gun**, which can be seen in the Artillery Hall, was aboard HMS *Royal George* when it sank in an accident off Portsmouth in 1782. It spent over 50 years underwater before being recovered. XIX.42

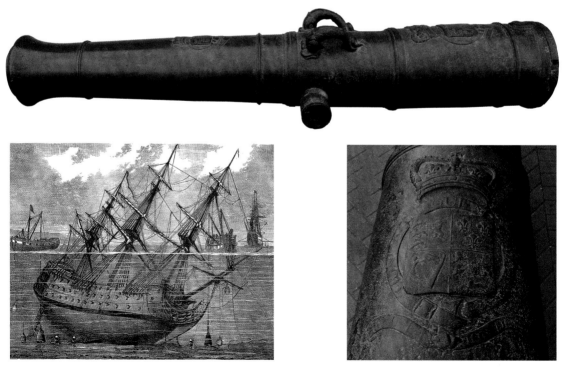

operator in Switzerland, found a way of casting a completely solid gun barrel out of bronze and then boring it out. This method, which provided a more truly-aligned bore, was rapidly taken up. In 1774 English industrialist John Wilkinson found a way to do the same with iron, and this soon became the standard method of production for Royal Navy guns. There were other small improvements too, such as the introduction of sights for better aim, flintlocks to fire the guns more reliably, and explosive shells (introduced in the 1840s) which allowed for the use of lighter guns.

Parade

◀ From Ranjit Singh's artillery train captured during the Sikh Wars in the 1840s, this field gun is complete with its original carriage and limber. XIX.329

7 This **Russian bronze siege gun**, dated 1793, was known as the **Licorne**, the French word for 'unicorn'. It was designed to fire explosive shells, one of several incremental improvements in the field of artillery during the period from the sixteenth century (when only mortars could fire exploding shells) to the late eighteenth century. XIX.815

▲ William Armstrong, Baron Armstrong, about 1895, *Navy and Army Illustrated*.

A nineteenth-century revolution

The late 1850s saw a major revolution in artillery design, as Victorian engineers brought a more rigorous scientific approach to the art of gun-making. Irish innovators Robert Mallet and Alexander Blakely led the way, carrying out mathematical analysis of gun barrels and the stresses to which they were subjected. They found, for example, that creating a stronger gun barrel was not simply a question of casting it more thickly. Instead, it was necessary to build up the barrel in layers, each calculated to take its share of the stress of firing.

The other major step forward was inspired by improvements in the accuracy and range of small-arms. This had been achieved by cutting spiral grooves into their barrels – a device known as rifling – in order to impart spin to a projectile. These 'rifles', as the new type of small-arms became known, proved to be so much more effective that they quickly replaced traditional smooth-bore muskets.

The potential to apply the same production technique to artillery was not lost on Victorian gun-makers, and by 1859 the first rifled artillery – designed by Sir William, later Lord, Armstrong – had entered service in the British Army. Indeed, the rifled, breech-loading Armstrong gun, with barrels built up in layers for extra strength, was hailed as the 'Wonder Gun' in Britain. It was not without its problems, however, not least because Armstrong decided not to incorporate steel into his design, despite the fact that it was now available in industrial quantities.

24 *See site map, inside front cover.* Outside Fort Nelson stands the impressive 42-ton bulk of a siege mortar known as **Mallet's Mortar**, after its designer Robert Mallet. Mortars of this type were the first British artillery pieces to be 'built up' in layers – in this case the wrought-iron powder chamber, which was strong enough to propel a shell of up to 2,986 lbs (1,351 kg). XIX.286
© Jonty Wilde

With the advent of rifled gun barrels, artillery technology advanced at such a pace – and with such widespread adoption among the main European military powers – that it revolutionised the nature of warfare. Indeed, the story of Fort Nelson itself provides a perfect illustration. In 1861, when work began on the site, it was expected to be a crucial part of the defence for Britain's premier naval base. In 1871, when the fortification was completed, it already faced vastly improved enemy artillery (see pages 12-31 for more on the Story of Fort Nelson).

More advances followed in quick succession, as a newly united Germany sparked an arms race between Europe's competing military powers. Most notable was the development of the recoil mechanism, which allowed the gun's barrel to slide back within the carriage when shot. This movement, which was managed by the use of hydraulics, meant that the gun was better able to absorb the shock of firing and did not throw itself out of position with every round. This in turn meant that the gun did not have to be re-laid between rounds, so allowing firing to be faster and more accurate.

The contribution of recoil mechanisms, allied to better range-finding and sighting devices meant that in the 1890s, heavy breech-loading rifled guns could throw projectiles weighing half a ton to a range of 10 miles or more. Further improvements such as the introduction of brass cartridge cases and 'smokeless' nitrocellulose powder instead of gunpowder contributed to the development of vast arsenals of so-called 'Quick-Firing' guns. As a new century dawned, the technology was in place to unleash a terrible new form of war.

The Story of Fort Nelson

▼ Manufacture of an Armstrong gun at Woolwich Arsenal. Finish-turning a 100-pounder. *Illustrated London News*, 5 April 1862.

8 In the gallery on 'Why Fort Nelson was built' you can see this example of a **40-pounder rifled breech-loading Armstrong gun,** manufactured in the middle of the nineteenth century. Weapons of this type were hailed as 'wonder guns' when they were first introduced. XIX.530

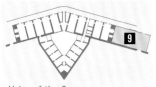

Voice of the Guns

The First World War

When the First World War began in 1914, Germany faced the prospect of having to fight a war on two fronts – against France in the west and Russia in the east. To avoid this, the Germans attempted to achieve the rapid defeat of France by advancing through Belgium, whose neutrality had long been guaranteed by Britain. This meant taking on and destroying the forts designed to defend Belgium's borders, which in turn meant the deployment of huge siege guns such as the monstrous Krupp 42-cm 'Big Bertha' – named after the gun manufacturing family's matriarch Bertha von Krupp.

After this initial onslaught, the early months of the war were characterised by fast-moving field operations, in which both sides made full use of their modern quick-firing artillery. An example of the German 7.7-cm Quick-Firing Field Gun can be seen in the Artillery Hall, close to the famous French equivalent – the 'Soixante-Quinze'. Guns like these caused massive casualties on both sides, and prevented either side outflanking the other so that the Western Front came to extend all the way from the French coast to the mountains of Switzerland.

Stalemate ensued, and as men on both sides sought shelter from the relentless artillery fire, they began to dig down into the ground around them. By the end of December 1914, these rudimentary defensive measures had evolved into a network of trenches, with the Germans proving especially skilled in their construction. What had started out as a fast-moving field operation had become a gigantic mutual siege.

Heavy bombardments of enemy lines were punctuated by poorly planned infantry attacks, and given the industrial power of modern weapons, these tactical errors resulted in horrifying numbers of casualties.

9 Much of the artillery deployed during the First World War fell into two categories: field guns which fired rounds at low angles, and howitzers which fired rounds at high angles. Eventually the Germans devised a gun and carriage which could combine these two roles – the **10.5-cm Quick-Firing Light Field Howitzer 16**, an example of which can be seen up close in the Voice of the Guns gallery. XIX.532

Efforts to break this appalling deadlock saw both sides employ new technology and weaponry. Great advances were made in aircraft design, for example, with airships and planes flown on reconnaissance, artillery-spotting and some bombing missions. Tanks too were introduced to the battlefield, armed with small quick-firing guns or machine guns.

Both developments presented new challenges to gunners on the ground. Special anti-aircraft guns had to be introduced, at first by improvisation – for example by placing a quick-firing field gun on a lorry for mobility. Against tanks, the challenge was to produce new anti-tank projectiles so that field guns could be effectively deployed to pierce their armour.

It became an all-enveloping war of machines and men on the battlefield, and immense industrial effort on both sides to keep feeding the front with guns and ammunition. The role of artillery in the new combined arms operations of 1918 was crucial. It was enabled by technical improvements in target identification, tactical improvements such as counter-battery fire and overhead fire (the 'creeping barrage') and logistical improvements that ensured field artillery fire could be massed where it was most needed and integrated with aircraft, armoured vehicles and infantry. The First World War proved to be the last war in which artillery was undoubtedly the chief battle winner.

Artillery Hall

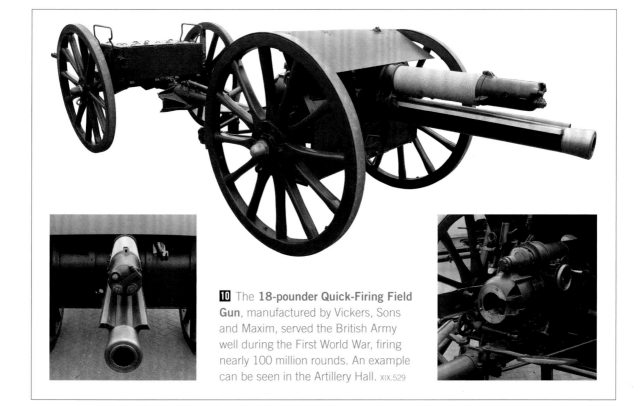

🔟 The **18-pounder Quick-Firing Field Gun**, manufactured by Vickers, Sons and Maxim, served the British Army well during the First World War, firing nearly 100 million rounds. An example can be seen in the Artillery Hall. XIX.529

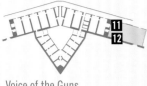

Voice of the Guns

The Second World War

The twenty years that separate the First and Second World Wars saw the nature of warfare change again. Air power became key, as bombers were developed to mount long-range missions over enemy territory and fast-moving fighters deployed to protect them from aerial attack. This in turn saw advances in anti-aircraft defences, for which high velocity shells were developed with reliable time fuzes. Directed by sophisticated fire control – itself aided by the invention of radar – this enabled land and naval gunners to hit airborne targets despite their rapid movement in three dimensions.

11 The original design of this **British 3.7-inch anti-aircraft gun** was the result of a competition between the Woolwich gun factory and Vickers Armstrong Ltd (won by the latter). XIX.840

© Jonty Wilde

On the ground, anti-tank guns also evolved to meet the threat of ever more heavily armoured tanks. Again, this meant using high-velocity shells to generate the power needed to penetrate the tanks' defences, but it also meant making anti-tank guns more mobile and easy to conceal so that they could avoid destruction by their intended targets. The British 25-pounder quick-firing field gun howitzer, of the type you can see fired on the Parade, performed such a role, and the Germans even targeted tanks with their mighty '88' anti-aircraft gun that you can see in the Voice of the Guns gallery. The war also saw the development of self-propelled artillery, capable of much improved all-terrain mobility. One of the best examples is the Sexton 25-pounder self-propelled gun that you can find in the Artillery Hall.

12 The **German '88'** was arguably the most famous artillery weapon of the Second World War – thanks to a determined German propaganda campaign and to its fearsome performance against allied tanks and aircraft. XIX.331

Artillery Hall

▶ 25-pounder self propelled gun – Sexton SPG on the Parade during a special event. XIX.527

13 This **German 7.5-cm/3.7-cm Pak 41 anti-tank gun** is a good example of the advances made to counter tank technology. Its tapered barrel allowed for the use of a large cartridge to power a small aerodynamic armour-piercing projectile through the muzzle at high velocity. The 7.5-cm Pak 41 was one of the last anti-tank guns brought into service by the German Army during the Second World War. It was designed to supplant the Pak 40 but only around 150 were ever built. AL.223

Although aircraft bombing missions reduced the importance of heavy artillery, big guns still had a role to play in the Second World War. Many were deployed for coastal defence – by the Germans along the Atlantic Wall, and by the British along the Channel. Indeed, many redundant naval guns were hastily emplaced as anti-invasion weapons after the fall of France in 1940.

The final months of the war in Europe saw the advent of new weapons such as the German V1 flying bomb and V2 rocket. Then came the detonation of the atomic bomb – first over Hiroshima on 6 August 1945 then over Nagasaki three days later. Together these terrifying new weapons not only heralded the end of the war, but appeared to usher in a future form of warfare in which artillery would no longer have a significant role to play. The reality has proved somewhat different.

14 The **British 5.5-inch gun howitzer**, with its distinctive vertical 'horns', was first used in North Africa at El Alamein. Though only a medium-sized gun, it was capable of lifting the turret from the most heavily armoured German tank. AL.1915

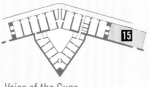

Voice of the Guns

The Cold War and after

Conventional artillery has remained a potent force on the battlefield despite the advent of the nuclear age. In fact, during the Cold War, much of the perceived Soviet threat to the West lay in its large army and vast arsenal of artillery, which always seemed poised to storm across Europe from the East.

In other respects, however, the use of artillery has dwindled. Most maritime nations have abandoned the use of big guns for coastal defence, for example, and attempts to engage aircraft using gunnery have been largely abandoned, with good reason, in favour of highly effective missiles.

15 Towering over you as you enter the Voice of the Guns gallery are two sections of the barrel for the '**Supergun**' commissioned by Iraqi leader Saddam Hussein in the 1980s. Designed by British engineer Gerald Bull, the finished gun would have boasted 26 such sections, making up a 156-metre long barrel. It would have been capable of sending a projectile weighing between 1 and 2 tons into temporary orbit. XIX.842-3 © Jonty Wilde

It is on land that gunnery has continued to make a contribution to military success – thanks to the various improvements made possible by modern technology: computers have been introduced for fire control; nuclear shells have been developed; new materials have enabled the construction of lighter guns that can be air-lifted by helicopter; recoilless guns have been further developed to become portable anti-tank weapons; and there have been general improvements in range, accuracy and hitting power – always the watchwords for artillerymen down the ages.

Much then has changed since the first projectiles were fired so many centuries ago, but it seems likely that artillery – the 'final argument of kings' as King Louis XIV of France put it – will continue to be part of the world's military future. Its story is not over yet.

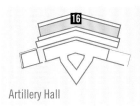

Artillery Hall

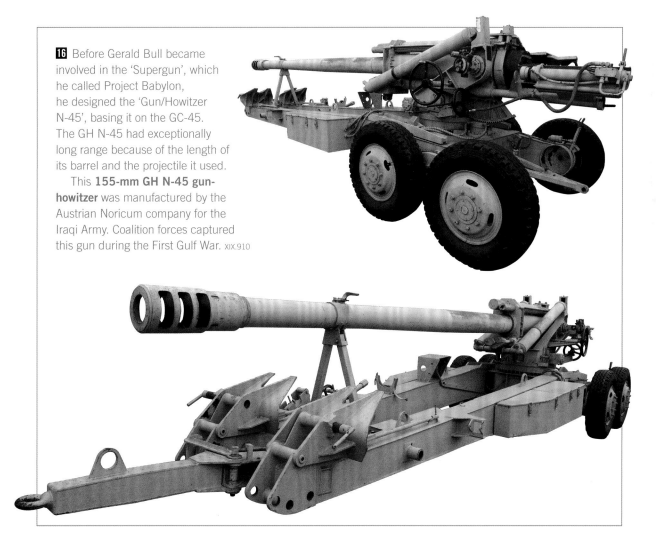

16 Before Gerald Bull became involved in the 'Supergun', which he called Project Babylon, he designed the 'Gun/Howitzer N-45', basing it on the GC-45. The GH N-45 had exceptionally long range because of the length of its barrel and the projectile it used.

This **155-mm GH N-45 gun-howitzer** was manufactured by the Austrian Noricum company for the Iraqi Army. Coalition forces captured this gun during the First Gulf War. XIX.910

Visitor information

We aim to make your visit to Fort Nelson as enjoyable as possible, and we offer a variety of other ways for you to extend your experience both during and after your visit.

OPENING TIMES

April to October, daily, 10am – 5pm
November to March, daily, 10am – 4pm
(closed 24-26 December)

ENQUIRIES

For further information about Fort Nelson, please call the visitor centre on 01329 848532, email fnenquiries@armouries.org.uk or visit www.royalarmouries.org

DISABLED ACCESS

The Royal Armouries welcomes visitors with disabilities. We offer accessible parking close to the main entrance of the site, and we have wheelchairs available for booking in advance of your visit (please call 01329 848511). We also permit access to guide dogs and assistance dogs. As a Scheduled Ancient Monument, there are some physical aspects of Fort Nelson that cannot be altered, such as steps of varying widths and heights, and changes of surface from paving stones to gravel and grass. However, we have installed a lift and ramps to provide access to most parts of the site.

EVENTS

We run a busy programme of events and activities throughout the year, including commemorative gun firings, talks about the fort and various types of family fun. To see our full programme and to book your tickets, visit www.royalarmouries.org

EDUCATION

The members of our dedicated education team run a variety of hands-on learning sessions and workshops for pupils of all ages. For more information, email education.fn@armouries.org.uk

CHILDREN

Fort Nelson, with its mix of tunnels, ramparts and galleries, is a fun place to explore. We also offer free treasure boxes for our youngest visitors, which feature a selection of toys, stories and activities designed to bring the site to life. For more information, just ask at the visitor centre.

GUIDED TOURS

We offer daily guided tours of the fort at 11.15am and 1.30pm. Each tour lasts about 50 minutes: a small charge is levied for adults, while under-16s go free. Tickets can be booked on arrival at the visitor centre.

PALMERSTON FORTS SOCIETY

The Palmerston Forts Society was formed in 1984 to help with the restoration and interpretation of Fort Nelson. When the site was taken over by the Royal Armouries, the society was encouraged to form the Portsdown Artillery Volunteers, who can be seen recreating the activities of the fort's original garrison and firing the fort's Victorian-era guns. If you are interested to find out more about the society or to join it, please email enquiries@palmerstonfortssociety.org.uk or visit www.palmerstonfortssociety.org.uk

EATING

Café 1871 is the perfect place to meet up with family and friends before, during or after exploring the fort. Situated in the visitor centre, it offers free Wi-Fi and a seasonal menu of light meals, delicious cakes, freshly brewed tea and barista-style coffee – all of which can be savoured indoors or outdoors, where you can enjoy some of the best views in southern Hampshire.

SHOPPING

Our museum shop is located in the visitor centre and is packed with unusual gifts for all ages, including specialist artillery publications, exquisitely crafted replica swords, locally brewed Hampshire beer, confectionery and toys. For an even wider selection of gifts, you can also shop online at shop.royalarmouries.org

GUN-FIRING EXPERIENCE

If you or one of your family and friends would like to get even closer to the big guns of Fort Nelson, we offer the chance for you to fire our Second World War Quick-Firing 25-Pounder Field Gun and explore the fort with our experts. Vouchers are available for three different types of gun-firing experience, which you can buy in the museum shop or online at shop.royalarmouries.org.

VENUE HIRE

Our fully restored Victorian fort and scenic position above the Solent combine to make Fort Nelson one of Hampshire's most unique, characterful and attractive venues for corporate and private hire. For more information, please call 01329 848518 or email fnfunctions@armouries.org.uk

SUPPORT US

Entrance to Fort Nelson is free, but we welcome donations of any size to support our work. As a charity, we can guarantee that every pound and penny donated is invested back into the museum, helping us to care for our collections and keep admission free for everyone. Thank you for your generosity.

ABOUT THE ROYAL ARMOURIES

The Royal Armouries is the United Kingdom's national museum of arms and armour, and one of the most important museums of its type in the world.

We have a long history, dating from the Middle Ages. Our celebrated core collection originated in the nation's working arsenal, which was assembled over many centuries at the Tower of London. The fact that objects were displayed to the public in Queen Elizabeth I's reign (1558-1603) makes us heir to one of the first deliberately devised visitor attractions in the country.

Our collection of about 75,000 items – excluding approximately 2,700 loans to other bodies – is now displayed and housed in our historic home at the White Tower in the Tower of London but also at our purpose-built museum in Leeds, and at Fort Nelson. Together these three sites attract over two million visitors every year.

In 2005 the museum acquired the former Ministry of Defence Pattern Room reference collection, originally started to govern the manufacture of military arms and armour. This collection began at the Tower of London, like that of the Royal Armouries, but then moved to the Royal Small Arms Factory at Enfield. The bulk of it is now housed at the National Firearms Centre, Leeds.

To find out more about our work, please visit royalarmouries.org.

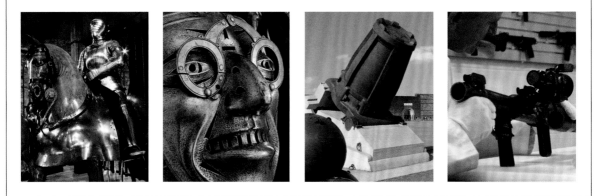

Front cover: 64-pounder Palliser rifled muzzle-loading gun. xix.253

Pages 4-5: 14-inch battle ship gun – Vickers-Armstrong Mk. VII Naval gun. xix.915

Inside back cover: A uniformed detachment from the Portsdown Artillery Volunteers firing a 16-pounder RML field gun on the Parade.

Back cover: Mallet's Mortar. xix.286. Quote: 'The Voice of the Guns' by Captain Gilbert Frankau, Royal Field Artillery, 1916.

Published by Royal Armouries Museum, Armouries Drive, Leeds LS10 1LT, United Kingdom

www.royalarmouries.org

Copyright © 2018 Trustees of the Royal Armouries

ISBN 978 0 94809 291 6

Edited by Martyn Lawrence

Designed by Geraldine Mead

Text by Jonathan Asbury, with thanks to Nick Hall

Principle photographers: Jacob Bishop, Gary Ombler

Photography on pages 2-3 © Aerial Photography Services

Photography on page 11 of German '88' and Iraqi 'Supergun' © Jonty Wilde

Maps on inside front cover and location plans by Graham Moores

Illustrations on pages 52 and 54 by Jeffrey Burn

Printed by W&G Baird

10 9 8 7 6 5 4 3 2 1

A CIP record for this book is available from the British Library